GREAT EXPEDITIONS

TO THE HEART OF
AFRICA

by VALERIE BODDEN

CREATIVE EDUCATION

PUBLISHED BY Creative Education
P.O. Box 227, Mankato, Minnesota 56002
Creative Education is an imprint of The Creative Company
www.thecreativecompany.us

DESIGN AND PRODUCTION BY Ellen Huber
ART DIRECTION BY Rita Marshall
PRINTED BY Corporate Graphics
in the United States of America

PHOTOGRAPHS BY
Alamy (Apic, The Art Archive, Classic Image, Robert Fried,
North Wind Picture Archives, Pictorial Press Ltd, The Print Collector),
Corbis (Bettmann), Getty Images (Alessandro Abbonizio/AFP,
Apic, English School, Hulton Archive), History-map.com,
iStockphoto (Mike Bentley, Brandon Laufenberg, Ahmet Mert Onengut)

LIBRARY OF CONGRESS CATALOGING-IN-PUBLICATION DATA
Bodden, Valerie.
To the heart of Africa / by Valerie Bodden.
p. cm. — (Great expeditions)
Summary: A history of David Livingstone's 19th-century excursions into
the African interior, detailing the challenges encountered, the individuals involved,
the discoveries made, and how the expeditions left their mark upon the world.

ISBN 978-1-60818-066-0
1. Livingstone, David, 1813-1873—Juvenile literature. 2. Explorers—Africa, Southern—
Biography—Juvenile literature. 3. Explorers—Scotland—Biography—Juvenile literature.
4. Missionaries, Medical—Africa, Southern—Biography—Juvenile literature. I. Title.

DT1110.L58B63 2011
916.704'23092—dc22 2010033414
CPSIA: 110310 PO1383

First Edition
2 4 6 8 9 7 5 3 1

TABLE OF CONTENTS

Chapters

The Dark Continent *7*

Into the Heart *17*

From Sea to Sea *25*

Opening Up Africa *35*

Trans-Africa Expedition Profiles

David Livingstone *13*

Sekwebu *23*

Sekeletu *33*

Pitsane *41*

Expedition Journal Entries

"The Want of Books" *9*

"Curious Forms Grow Every Where" *19*

"Your Improvement as an Observer" *27*

"Effects of the Fever" *37*

Timeline *44*

Endnotes *45*

Selected Bibliography *46*

For Further Reading *47*

Index *48*

A MAP OF
AFRICA
TO ILLUSTRATE THE TRAVELS OF
LIVINGSTONE, STANLEY AND CAMERON.

Scale of English Miles.

Livingstone's Routes ———— Stanley's Do. ———— Cameron's Do. ----------

Stanford's Geog.l Estab.t 55, Charing Cro

THE DARK CONTINENT

———

FOR CENTURIES, PEOPLE KNEW LITTLE ABOUT THE LANDS BEYOND THEIR HOMES. BUT BY THE BEGINNING OF THE 1800S, THE KNOWN WORLD WAS BECOMING A BIGGER PLACE. MANY OF THE PLANET'S REMOTEST AND ONCE-INACCESSIBLE CORNERS WERE BEING EXPLORED BY ADVENTURERS FROM EUROPEAN COUNTRIES SUCH AS SPAIN, PORTUGAL, AND GREAT BRITAIN.

In fact, these nations and others had established COLONIES in North and South America, the WEST INDIES, Asia, and Australia. But there was one substantial landmass that remained largely a mystery: Africa. Although a handful of European trading posts and settlements had been planted along Africa's coasts, the interior of the continent was as yet unexplored. Unknown lands were colored black on maps of the day, earning Africa the nickname "The Dark Continent." During the mid-1800s, though, Scottish MISSIONARY and explorer David Livingstone crossed Africa's interior and brought word of the lands he had discovered back to fascinated leaders in Europe, who would

By the end of the 19th century, Africa had been explored by at least three famous, British-born explorers, including David Livingstone.

soon change the landscape of the continent by carving it into pieces among themselves.

Long before Livingstone first set foot in Africa in 1841, Europeans had shown an interest in the continent. During the 15th century, PRINCE HENRY THE NAVIGATOR of Portugal had sent naval expeditions along the western coast of Africa, and 26 years after his death in 1460, the Portuguese successfully sailed around the Cape of Good Hope, at the southern end of the continent, and began to explore East Africa. As the Portuguese traveled along the coastlines, they established settlements and forts, from which they shipped African goods such as gold and salt back to their homeland.

Soon, the British, Dutch, and French had also established a number of trading posts on the West African coast. These posts enabled a lucrative trade—not only in goods but also in African people—to begin. In most cases, European traders did not capture slaves themselves but bought them from native Africans, who, when warring with other tribes, made slaves of their captives and marched them to the coast. In return for their human merchandise, African slave traders were given European goods such as copper kettles, cloth, and guns. By the late 1500s and early 1600s, most of the slaves purchased with such goods were being sent by European traders to North and South America and to the Caribbean, where they were put to work on sugar cane and cotton plantations and in mines. On the eastern coast of Africa, a separate slave trade thrived, with Arab and Portuguese slavers sending slaves to ARABIA, India, and China. Although the British abolished slavery throughout their empire in 1834 and attempted to enforce a blockade of departing slave ships—belonging to any nation—more than 60,000 slaves a year were still being shipped to Brazil, Cuba, and North America by the 1850s.

Late in the 1800s, British police began to arrest those who persisted in selling slaves, such as these Arab-African traders.

EXPEDITION JOURNAL

DAVID LIVINGSTONE
November 1853 journal entry

I feel the want of books in this journey more than anything else. A Sechuana [Setswana] PENTATEUCH, *a lined journal,* Thomson's Tables, *a Nautical Almanack, and a Bible, constitute my stock. The last constitutes my chief resource; but the want of other mental pabulum [intellectual nourishment] is felt severely. There is little to interest in the conversation of the people. Loud disputes often about the women [of the villages], and angry altercations in which the same string of abuse is used, are more frequent than anything else.*

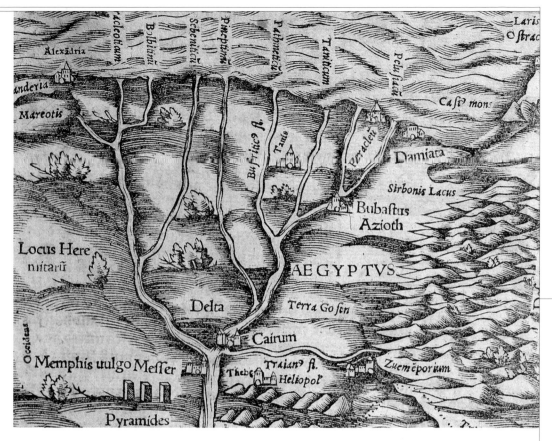

Even as a steady stream of slaves was being shipped out of Africa, most Europeans remained ignorant of what the interior of this vast continent—the second-largest on the planet, after Asia—might hold. Locations only 100 miles (161 km) inland went unexplored, and nearly nothing was known of the landscape between the Sahara Desert in the north and the British (formerly Dutch) Cape Colony in the far south. Most Europeans believed that central Africa consisted of an immense, inhospitable desert. East Africa's Nile River—well-known in northern lands such as Egypt—remained a mystery in the south, and some mapmakers speculated that it began in a fabled range of peaks that they called the Mountains of the Moon. Some maps even depicted another of the continent's major rivers—West Africa's Niger River—as flowing backwards, from east to west.

Parts of the Nile River were known to Europeans of the 1500s (as mapped above), but the wild waters continued to fascinate people well into the 1800s (opposite).

Europeans' ignorance was due not to a lack of interest in the continent but to an inability to explore it. Africa's dangers were many. A mysterious disease, then called African fever (today known as MALARIA), could sicken and even kill an entire expedition of otherwise healthy men. Animals such as lions, rhinoceroses, and snakes could attack explorers, and native tribes sometimes proved to be hostile, especially if not presented with a TRIBUTE. Waterfalls and rapids made many of Africa's rivers dangerous or unnavigable. Overland travel could be blocked by dense jungles, and floods during the rainy season (June to September in the west, October to April in the south, and much of the year in the rainforests of Central Africa) turned otherwise dry ground into swamps. The temperature—which often exceeded 100 °F (38 °C) during the dry season—would take a toll on both men and their equipment, from scientific instruments to signal rockets to even pencils. And that equipment would have to be transported almost entirely by humans, since the TSETSE FLY abounded throughout much of the continent, infecting horses, oxen, and other livestock that might otherwise have been used as pack animals with deadly diseases.

The dreaded diseases carried by tsetse flies (above) caused many missionary families such as the Livingstones (opposite) to leave Africa.

Despite such dangers and difficulties, some adventurous Europeans did attempt to penetrate the African interior during the 15th and 16th centuries. Many died trying. In 1788, British naturalist Sir Joseph Banks established the Association for Promoting the Discovery of the Interior Parts of Africa, also known as the African

TRANS-AFRICA EXPEDITION PROFILE:
DAVID LIVINGSTONE

David Livingstone was born in Blantyre, Scotland, on March 19, 1813. Because his family was poor, Livingstone began to work in Blantyre's cotton mills when he was only 10 years old. After putting in a 12-hour workday, the boy attended the company school from 8:00 to 10:00 P.M. and then went home to read. In his spare time, Livingstone roamed the countryside, carefully studying rocks, trees, and plants. After becoming a doctor and a missionary, Livingstone traveled to Africa in 1841 and spent 28 of his remaining 32 years on that continent. During Livingstone's final years in Africa, he sent no communications, and several search parties were sent to find him. He was finally located by American journalist Henry Morton Stanley in 1871. Livingstone chose to remain in Africa, where he died in 1873 at the age of 60.

Association. The organization's first expedition failed before it even began, however, when its leader, American John Ledyard, died in Cairo, Egypt. Other explorers who traveled to the continent during the late 18th and early 19th centuries—including Scotsmen Mungo Park and Hugh Clapperton, and Englishman Richard Lander—also died during their travels.

In the early 19th century, Christian missionaries joined the ranks of explorers and adventurers making inroads in Africa. They traveled from England, France, America, and other countries

Some missionaries to Africa, such as David Livingstone, enjoyed good relationships with the native people and were welcomed into their villages.

to minister to the African natives. In the Cape Colony alone, there were 80 mission settlements by 1841. A few other mission stations were scattered outside the colony's borders. Most missionaries were sponsored by organizations such as the London Missionary Society. Among the Society's remotest stations was Kuruman, a settlement located about 600 miles (965 km) north of Cape Town (on the southern coast) that had been founded by Robert Moffat in 1821. Twenty years later, a new missionary, freshly graduated from the Society's seminary, joined Moffat at Kuruman. Few could have guessed then that young David Livingstone was embarking on an adventure that would soon reveal some of the best-kept secrets of the African interior.

INTO THE HEART

———

IN 1834, 21-YEAR-OLD DAVID LIVINGSTONE DECIDED THAT HE WANTED TO BECOME A MEDICAL MISSIONARY. WHILE WORKING PART-TIME AT THE COTTON MILLS WHERE HE HAD BEEN EMPLOYED SINCE THE AGE OF 10, IN 1836 HE BEGAN STUDYING MEDICINE AT WHAT WAS THEN KNOWN AS ANDERSON'S COLLEGE IN GLASGOW, SCOTLAND. TWO YEARS LATER, WHILE

continuing his medical training, Livingstone was accepted into the London Missionary Society, and in November 1840, he was licensed as a doctor and ordained as a missionary. Although his original intention had been to travel to China to establish a ministry there, the ongoing FIRST OPIUM WAR derailed his plans, and he decided instead to go to South Africa.

On December 8, 1840, Livingstone boarded the wooden sailing ship *George* for the three-month voyage to Cape Town. Soon after arriving in Africa, Livingstone headed for Kuruman, traveling by ox wagon over the sandy landscape. Upon his arrival in late July, he began studying Setswana, the language of the

———

After Livingstone arrived in Africa, he wanted to explore it and devoted much of his later life to studying the Zambezi River and its environs.

native Tswana people. As quickly as Livingstone became fluent in the language, he also grew tired of his assignment, since so few of the people he encountered seemed interested in the gospel he preached. His frustration with settled mission life led Livingstone to request permission from the London Missionary Society to "go forward into the dark interior" to scout for prospective mission sites among unreached tribes.

The Society agreed to Livingstone's request, and he soon set out on a series of trips to the north of Kuruman, eventually leaving the settlement altogether and establishing a new mission station among a Tswana group known as the Bakhatla in 1843. He later moved farther north to minister to the Kwena, another Tswana tribe, in the village of Kolobeng, about 300 miles (483 km) from Kuruman.

While Livingstone continued to labor as a missionary to the Kwena (among whom he made his only convert, a tribal chief named Sechele), he began to dream of traveling even farther north. He again wrote to the Society, saying this time that he wanted to bring Christianity to all of the tribes in the area. Missionary zeal was not Livingstone's only motivation, however; he also wanted to locate an unknown lake, which the natives called Ngami. In August 1849, Livingstone—along with BIG-GAME hunters William Cotton Oswell and Mungo Murray—became one of the first Europeans to see the lake. In 1850 and 1851, Livingstone took two more trips to the north of Kolobeng, this time bringing along his wife, Mary Moffat (daughter of Robert Moffat), whom he had married in 1845, and their three young children. (Two more children would be born during the journeys, but one would die.)

During their 1851 travels, Livingstone and his companions were stunned by the sight of the wide, powerful Zambezi River, which they reached near the middle of its course. Although a Portuguese explorer named Silva Porto had already discovered the river in 1847–48, few people in Europe were aware of this fact, and Livingstone willingly took credit as being the first white man to reach the Zambezi, despite later learning of Porto's discovery. The river excited Livingstone not only because of its massive size—300 to 600 yards (275–549 m) across at this stretch—and strong current but also because it was most likely the same river that flowed into the sea in Mozambique,

EXPEDITION JOURNAL

David Livingstone

December 1853 (from Missionary Travels and Researches in South Africa)

We spent a Sunday on our way up to the confluence of the Leeba and Leeambye [Zambezi]. Rains had fallen here before we came, and the woods had put on their gayest hue. Flowers of great beauty and curious forms grow every where; they are unlike those in the south, and so are the trees. Many of the forest-tree leaves are palmated and largely developed; the trunks are covered with lichens, and the abundance of ferns which appear in the woods shows we are now in a more humid climate.... The ground begins to swarm with insect life; and in the cool, pleasant mornings the welkin [sky] rings with the singing of birds.... The notes here, however, strike the mind by their loudness and variety, as the wellings forth from joyous hearts of praise to Him who fills them with overflowing gladness. All of us rise early to enjoy the luscious balmy air of the morning.

a country located on Africa's eastern coast. This river presented the possibility of opening a "highway" through the interior of the African continent. Livingstone believed that if European traders could use this waterway for commerce, the slave trade would eventually come to an end, and Africans would turn away from old customs to embrace Christianity. Invigorated by his discovery and eager to learn whether the Zambezi was navigable along its entire course, Livingstone took his family back to Cape Town and from there sent them home to Britain. Then he set out to plan his greatest adventure yet—a cross-continental tour of the Zambezi River.

Livingstone's expedition faced such dangers as being capsized by territorial hippopotamuses while riding boats down the Zambezi.

More than a decade of living in and traveling through southern Africa had introduced Livingstone to the rigors of exploration on the continent, and he began to gather supplies with his previous experiences in mind. He packed muskets for shooting the big game he knew was abundant and could be relied upon as his party's main food supply. Other rations included biscuits, a few pounds of tea and sugar, and 20 pounds (9 kg) of coffee. For those times when food ran low, Livingstone carried a supply of beads to trade with the natives. A small tin crate, about 15 inches (38 cm) long on each side, was packed with spare clothing, and another crate carried medicines. Livingstone also packed books such as a nautical almanac and *Thomson's Logarithm Tables* (both of which would help him determine his position on land based on the positions of heavenly bodies such as stars) and his Bible, as well as scientific instruments, including a thermometer, compass, and SEXTANT. To improve his mapmaking skills, Livingstone spent

time studying with Sir Thomas Maclear, the Royal Astronomer at the Cape of Good Hope.

With his preparations made, Livingstone left Cape Town on June 8, 1852, and headed for Linyanti, a village populated by the Kololo people, whom Livingstone had met on earlier journeys to the north. After stopping for a few months at Kuruman, Livingstone first skirted the Kalahari Desert, where temperatures at times topped 125 °F (52 °C), then cut his way through dense forests, and finally waded through a nearly impenetrable swamp to reach Linyanti (in present-day Botswana) by May 1853.

At Linyanti, the Kololo received Livingstone warmly, and their king, Sekeletu, agreed to provide 160 porters for Livingstone's journey. In return, Livingstone pledged to open up trade to the area and to eventually establish a new mission station among the Kololo, which Sekeletu believed would help secure peace with the nearby Ndebele people, whom Livingstone's father-in-law had earlier befriended. With these potential benefits of friendship in mind, Sekeletu offered to accompany Livingstone on the first phase of the trip, during which the explorer hoped to find a suitable location for the new mission station. At the end of June 1853, Livingstone and his large entourage of natives set out from Linyanti toward the Zambezi River.

TRANS-AFRICA EXPEDITION PROFILE:
SEKWEBU

Captured by the Ndebele as a young boy, Sekwebu had spent time living near Tete, Mozambique, and had already made several trips along the Zambezi when he met Livingstone. King Sekeletu personally selected Sekwebu to serve as Livingstone's interpreter and leader of the natives during the journey from Linyanti to Mozambique, and Livingstone considered him a "person of great prudence and sound judgment." The explorer wrote that if it had not been for Sekwebu's "good sense, tact, and command of the language of the tribes through which we passed," the party may not have succeeded in reaching the coast. Upon arriving in Quelimane in 1856, Livingstone invited Sekwebu to accompany him to England, but the frightened native jumped off their ship and drowned.

FROM SEA TO SEA

AFTER LEAVING LINYANTI, LIVINGSTONE AND HIS PARTY JOURNEYED NORTH TO THE ZAMBEZI, WHERE THEY OBTAINED LONG, NARROW, FLAT-BOTTOMED CANOES FROM THE VILLAGES ALONG THE RIVER AND BEGAN TO PADDLE UPSTREAM. AFTER COVERING 300 MILES (480 KM), LIVINGSTONE WAS DISAPPOINTED TO FIND THAT MALARIA WAS PREVALENT EVERYWHERE.

The explorer himself was struck by African fever eight times in four months. By September, he was forced to admit that no healthy location for a mission settlement existed along this stretch of the river, and he returned, discouraged, to Linyanti.

There Sekeletu outfitted Livingstone for the next phase of the journey, which would take him to the Portuguese territory of Angola on the western coast of the continent. The Kololo king provided Livingstone with 27 men, led by one of his most trusted tribal chiefs, Pitsane. Sekeletu also gave the explorer his own canoe, several oxen, and as much food as the men could carry.

The canoes Livingstone used were dug out from large, straight trees found in the region along the river such as ebony or sausage trees.

On November 11, 1853, Livingstone left Linyanti and again returned to the Zambezi. The party slowly made their way up the river through present-day Zambia, paddling carefully through the shallow water and rapids in order to keep their craft from overturning. Although navigation would have been easier in the deeper waters toward the middle of the river, the party remained close to shore for fear of hippopotamuses, which could tip them out into the water.

As they traveled, Livingstone and his native porters quickly fell into a routine. Each day, they rose at 5:00 A.M. and paddled until 11:00 A.M., when the party stopped for a lunch of leftover meat or a biscuit with honey and then set out again in the oppressive heat of the day. Two hours before sunset, they stopped for a dinner of bread or freshly caught game, after which Livingstone's traveling companions set up his tent and bed, started a fire nearby, and built their own open-fronted shelters in a circle facing the fire. Each night, Livingstone wrote in his journal, carefully recording measurements of temperature, rainfall, and position. He took note of unusual birds, flowers, and fish, once documenting a peculiar striped fish with sharp teeth that sometimes leaped into the party's canoes. In many cases, Livingstone believed he was describing species that were new to science, but since he had chosen not to haul along many reference books, he couldn't be sure.

By early 1854, Livingstone and his men had emerged from the lands controlled by the Kololo and reached the territory of the Lunda people. There they left the river (which would soon turn to the northeast) and began to travel overland. The rainy season had begun, and the party struggled to hack paths through the tangled jungle with axes. Game was scarce and difficult to track, and the men survived on plant material such as cassava until they reached the Lunda chief, Shinde, who provided the explorers with food.

As Livingstone and his party traveled beyond the Lunda toward the coast, Livingstone noted the increased evidence of the slave trade. He was horrified to learn that chiefs in the area often killed the leaders of weak villages and sold the women and children to traders. Tribes also became more hostile toward the travelers and demanded *hongo*, or payment—often in the form of oxen, ivory, guns, or slaves—before they would allow the party to pass. Livingstone refused to sell any of his men and, when hongo couldn't be avoided, offered ivory or an ox.

EXPEDITION JOURNAL

ROYAL ASTRONOMER SIR THOMAS MACLEAR
letter to Livingstone, March 27, 1854

It is both interesting and amusing to trace your improvement as an observer. Some of your early observations, as you remark, are rough, and the angles assigned to the objects misplaced in transcribing. But upon the whole I do not hesitate to assert that no explorer on record has determined his path with the precision you have accomplished. It is delightful to remark your cheerful tone midst so many difficulties, dangers and privations—your amusing anecdotes and happy knack of turning everything to the best account.

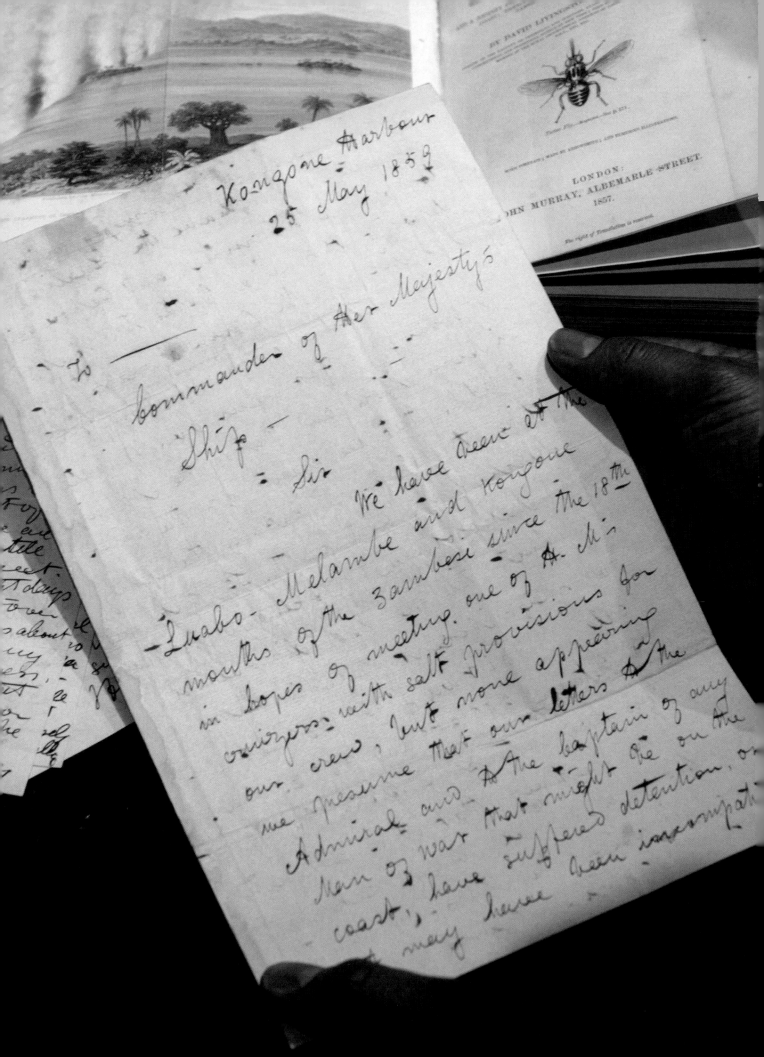

Kongone Harbour
25 May 1859

To ————

Commander of Her Majesty's

"Ship" ————

Sir

We have been at the
Luabo - Melambe and Kongone
mouths of the Zambesi since the 18th
in hopes of meeting one of H. M's
cruizers with salt provisions for
our crew, but none appearing
we presume that our letters to the
Admiral and to the captain of any
Man of war that might be on the
coast, have suffered detention, or
may have been _____

By early May 1854, the party was within 150 miles (240 km) of the coast when Livingstone, who had already suffered several bouts of malaria, became seriously ill. By the time he arrived at the coastal city of Loanda (now spelled "Luanda") on May 31, 1854, Livingstone could no longer walk and had to be carried by his companions. Fortunately, a British doctor aboard a warship in Loanda's harbor was able to help him. Not content to rest and recover fully, however, Livingstone soon began to make preparations to travel to the opposite side of the continent.

Livingstone wrote many letters throughout the various expeditions; some have managed to survive in legible condition to the present day.

Livingstone and his men set out again on September 20, 1854. Following much the same route as they had on the westward journey, the party this time traveled more slowly, held up by hostile tribes, floods, and poor health. A year later, in September 1855, they returned to Linyanti, where Sekeletu selected 114 men (some of whom had just completed the round-trip journey with Livingstone) to accompany the explorer to Portuguese-controlled Mozambique. An experienced Zambezi traveler named Sekwebu was appointed to lead them.

On November 3, 1855, Livingstone and his new party struck out for the Zambezi, which they now followed downstream, to the east. After traveling for two weeks, they came upon a spectacular waterfall on the border of present-day Zimbabwe and Zambia. The waterfall, which spanned more than a mile (1.6 km) and plunged more than 350 feet (107 m), was called *Mosi-oa-Tunya*, or "The Smoke That Thunders," by the natives. To honor the queen of his native Britain, Livingstone renamed it Victoria Falls.

The waters of the
5,500-foot-wide
(1,676 m) Victoria Falls
plunge into a chasm
and continue on
through a gorge that
leads to a deep pool
called the Boiling Pot.

Rather than continuing to follow the Zambezi as it looped south below Victoria Falls, Livingstone decided to travel overland across the Batoka PLATEAU in what is now Zambia. The grassy, open land was home to large game such as Cape buffalo, hartebeests (large antelope with ringed horns), elephants, and lions. Although he described the natives of the Batoka Plateau as being uncivilized and immoral, Livingstone believed he had at last found a safe, healthy location for the establishment of a European mission. Before Europeans could settle the area, however, Livingstone needed to make sure it could be reached by following the Zambezi from Mozambique. He decided to return to the river, arriving there in early 1856. Since they couldn't afford to purchase canoes, Livingstone and his men walked along the riverbanks, slowly picking their way through the thick underbrush.

Grass-eating Cape buffalo weigh around 1,000 pounds (454 kg) and prefer to live in savanna habitats that border rivers and lakes.

By February, Livingstone was growing anxious to reach the coast, and he decided to bypass a large bend in the river by striking off overland. When he again reached the Zambezi at the Portuguese settlement of Tete, Mozambique, in March, Livingstone was unaware that his shortcut had caused him to miss the Kebrabasa Rapids, a 30-mile-long (48 km) section of absolutely impassable falls and whitewater. He believed his dream of a fully navigable Zambezi was still alive.

TRANS-AFRICA EXPEDITION PROFILE: SEKELETU

Sekeletu, who became king of the Kololo around the age of 18, was instrumental in the success of Livingstone's cross-continental journey, providing the explorer with both men and supplies, free of charge. After Livingstone's journey, Sekeletu waited for the explorer to return as promised and help secure peace with the Ndebele so that the Kololo could move to a healthier location—one free of malaria. When Livingstone failed to return (except for a brief visit), Sekeletu's tribe went into a rapid decline. The king himself was afflicted with the contagious skin disease leprosy, and, believing it to be the result of witchcraft, killed large numbers of his own people. Soon after his 1863 death, the rest of the Kololo people were wiped out by disease and enemy attacks.

OPENING UP AFRICA

ON APRIL 22, 1856, LIVINGSTONE AND 8 OF HIS MEN STEPPED INTO CANOES FOR THE LAST 270 MILES (435 KM) OF THEIR JOURNEY TO THE COASTAL CITY OF QUELIMANE, MOZAMBIQUE. ALTHOUGH THIS PORTION OF THE EXPEDITION WAS LESS TAXING THAN ALMOST ANY PREVIOUS SECTION HAD BEEN, LIVINGSTONE WAS SICK WITH MALARIA FOR MUCH OF THE WAY.

Despite his illness, Livingstone was able to complete the trip, arriving at Quelimane on May 20 and becoming the first European to cross the African continent from coast to coast. It had been nearly 4 years and 6,000 miles (9,655 km) since he had left Cape Town to begin his explorations of the African interior.

When he arrived at the seaport, Livingstone learned that British warships had been stopping near the mouth of the Zambezi for several months to ask if he had arrived. In fact, the captain and crew of one ship that had approached to inquire about Livingstone had been killed when their vessel had been wrecked on a sandbar at the river's mouth. Two months after

In 1800s Africa, cities along major rivers and in natural seaports on the coasts became gathering places for people to trade goods and information.

Livingstone arrived in Quelimane, he boarded the British warship *Frolic* and began his journey home to England, accompanied by Sekwebu. The African, who had never before been on the sea, was overwhelmed by the new experience and jumped overboard, using the ship's anchor rope to pull himself under the water. His body was never found.

Saddened by Sekwebu's death, Livingstone nevertheless continued the journey to England, where he received a hero's welcome in London in early December 1856. The explorer had been able to send letters to England while in Loanda and Quelimane, letting the outside world know of his progress, and in 1854,

Livingstone documented the adventures, setbacks, and discoveries of his travels in his diary, filling several notebooks with his thoughts.

the London newspaper *The Times* had reported that Livingstone's expedition was "one of the greatest geographical explorations of the age." Everyone in Britain seemed to agree. Many considered him the world's greatest explorer, and he was so famous that only Queen Victoria—with whom he was able to meet privately—was better known among British subjects around the globe. In addition to being honored at official receptions, Livingstone was often mobbed by admirers on the street and even in church.

Although others considered his journey a success, Livingstone had mixed feelings about his travels. He feared that his geographical accomplishments would mean nothing if more missionaries and traders did not go to Africa. His concern stemmed from a letter he had received from the London Missionary Society before returning to England, which said that the many obstacles to traveling in the African interior would prevent new missions from being opened there in the foreseeable future.

EXPEDITION JOURNAL

DAVID LIVINGSTONE

May 1854 (from Missionary Travels and Researches in South Africa*)*

I felt much refreshed, and could then realize and meditate on the weakening effects of the fever. They were curious even to myself; for, though I had tried several times since we left Ngio to take lunar observations, I could not avoid confusion of time and distance, neither could I hold the instrument steady, nor perform a simple calculation.... Often, on getting up in the mornings, I found my clothing as wet from perspiration as if it had been dipped in water.... I forgot the days of the week and the names of my companions, and, had I been asked, I probably could not have told my own.... One day I supposed that I had got the true theory of it, and would certainly cure the next attack, whether in myself or companions; but some new symptoms would appear, and scatter all the fine speculations which had sprung up ... in one department of my brain.

THE LIFE & EXPLORATIONS
OF
DR. LIVINGSTONE

BORN AT BLANTYRE, MARCH, 19, 1813

DIED IN CENTRAL AFRICA, MAY 4, 1873

Hoping to encourage British interest in Africa, Livingstone wrote *Missionary Travels and Researches in South Africa* in 1857. The book became an instant best seller. He also embarked on a speaking tour of the country, encouraging Britons to bring commerce and Christianity to Africa. In May 1857, the London Missionary Society agreed to establish two new mission stations in central Africa. One was to be among the Kololo, with Livingstone as its head. Livingstone, however, had lost interest in serving as a missionary to the Kololo, and two other men, along with their wives and five children, were sent in his place. Although Livingstone had downplayed the seriousness of malaria in the area, writing that he "apprehended no great mortality among missionaries" as a result of the disease, within two months of their arrival, all but three of that party were dead.

Livingstone had turned down the missionary posting among the Kololo to pursue a government-sponsored exploration of the Zambezi, as he still hoped to develop the river into a highway across Africa. In 1858, Livingstone, along with 10 natives and 6 other Europeans—among them his younger brother Charles, geologist Richard Thornton, and physician John Kirk—set off upstream on the Zambezi from Mozambique, beginning a 6-year exploration of the river and its surrounding area. The expedition was largely considered a failure, however, as Livingstone at last discovered that the Kebrabasa Rapids were not navigable and failed to establish either commerce or Christianity on the continent.

Despite the failures of his expeditions, Livingstone's exploits were celebrated in book form during his lifetime and for many years after.

Determined to redeem himself after the failed Zambezi expedition, Livingstone returned to Africa in 1866, this time in search of the Nile River's source. For seven years, he journeyed across the continent, suffering through many illnesses along the way, before dying in a native village on May 1, 1873. Loyal natives carried his body from the interior of the continent to Bagamoyo, Tanzania, from where it was sent back to England.

In death, Livingstone was once again received as a hero in his country, and his call to open Africa to intercontinental trade, Christianity, and WESTERN civilization was finally answered. Explorers embarked on new expeditions across the continent, traders established new outposts, and missionaries set up new settlements. Soon, European governments were also setting their sights on Africa, and by the 1880s, several nations—including Britain, Belgium, Germany, Italy, Portugal, and France—were involved in a heated scramble to acquire more African colonies. By the end of the 19th century, almost the entire continent had been claimed by one European nation or another, often by force. It wasn't until the second half of the 20th century that most of these colonies would become independent countries.

Although he played an indirect role in helping to bring Africans under European rule, Livingstone also helped end the slave trade on the continent. During his journeys, Livingstone had often come into contact with slave traders. He had seen firsthand the cruelty inflicted on slaves, who were taken from their homes and marched across the continent in shackles. After his cross-continental expedition,

Trans-Africa Expedition Profile:
Pitsane

Pitsane, a trusted Kololo tribal chief, served as Livingstone's second-in-command during the journey from Linyanti to Angola. He ensured that the tribes along the Zambezi over which Sekeletu ruled provided the explorers with gifts of food, as ordered by the king. Upon returning to his people at the end of the journey, Pitsane delivered an hour-long speech, during which he enthusiastically reported on the kindness of the white men he had met and credited Livingstone with peacefully opening a trade route to the western coast. In 1860, Pitsane again joined Livingstone, this time escorting the explorer—who briefly visited the Kololo during his second Zambezi expedition—part of the way back to the eastern coast.

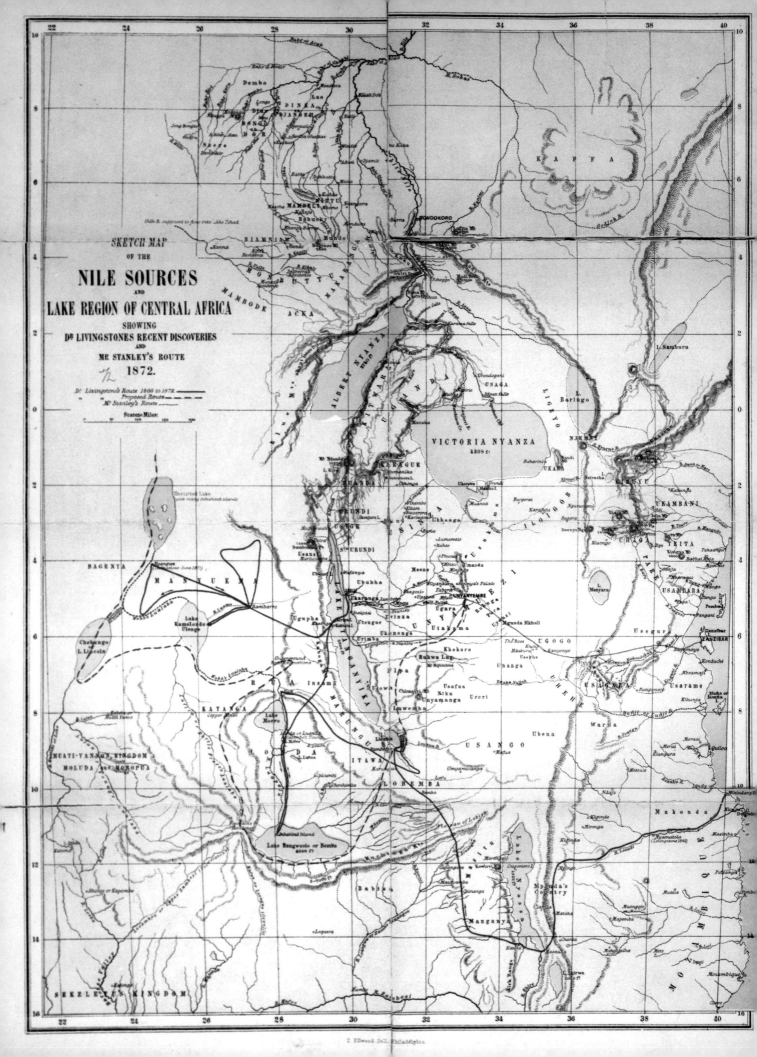

SKETCH MAP
OF THE
NILE SOURCES
AND
LAKE REGION OF CENTRAL AFRICA
SHOWING
Dr LIVINGSTONES RECENT DISCOVERIES
AND
Mr STANLEY'S ROUTE
1872.

Dr Livingstone's Route 1866 to 1872. ————
"   Proposed Route ——— ———
"   Mr Stanley's Route ——————

Statue Miles:

T. Ellwood Zell, Philadelphia.

Livingstone devoted much of his time to delivering speeches condemning the slave trade. He also wrote letters and journaled about the horrors of the trade, and these accounts helped to convince the British government to force an end to the practice by threatening the sultan of nearby ZANZIBAR with a naval blockade if the island's slave market wasn't closed. The sultan signed an agreement forbidding the sale of slaves in June 1873. Livingstone, who had died a month earlier, never saw the profound changes his explorations brought to Africa, but nearly a century and a half later, he is still recognized as the first explorer to shed light on the mysteries of this once-unknown continent.

Livingstone literally left his heart in Africa; the tree inscription that marked the spot where his heart was buried has since been moved to England.

TIMELINE

1813 — David Livingstone is born in Blantyre, Scotland, on March 19.

1823 — Livingstone begins laboring at a cotton mill.

1834 — Great Britain's Slavery Abolition Act takes effect in August, but slave trading continues.

1836 — Livingstone enrolls in Anderson's College in Glasgow, Scotland, to begin medical training.

1840 — Following his qualification as a doctor and his ordination as a missionary, Livingstone sets sail for South Africa on December 8.

1841 — In September, Livingstone embarks on the first of three journeys to the north from Kuruman.

1843 — Livingstone establishes a mission station among the Bakhatla tribe of the Tswana people.

1845 — Livingstone marries Mary Moffat on January 2 and later establishes a mission station among the Kwena.

1849 — Livingstone and companions William Cotton Oswell and Mungo Murray become the first Europeans to see Lake Ngami on August 1.

1851 — On August 4, Livingstone arrives at the Zambezi River, gaining credit for "discovering" it.

1852 — Livingstone sets out on June 8 for Linyanti, where he will begin his cross-continental journey.

1853 — After reaching Linyanti in May, Livingstone explores the Zambezi in hopes of finding a location for a new mission station.

1853 — On November 11, Livingstone and 27 native porters begin a 1,000-mile (1,610 km) journey to Angola.

1854 — An ailing Livingstone is carried into Loanda, Angola, by his native porters on May 31.

1854 — On September 20, Livingstone sets out from Loanda to return to Linyanti.

1855 — Livingstone departs from Linyanti for the Portuguese colony of Mozambique on November 3.

1855 — On November 17, Livingstone becomes the first European to see *Mosi-oa-Tunya*, which he renames Victoria Falls.

1856 — In February, Livingstone decides to bypass a bend of the Zambezi, missing the impassable Kebrabasa Rapids.

1856 — Livingstone arrives at the port of Quelimane, Mozambique, on May 20.

1856 — On July 12, Livingstone and Sekwebu board the *Frolic*, but Sekwebu jumps overboard a month later.

1856 — Livingstone arrives in England in early December and is greeted as a national hero.

1857 — *Missionary Travels and Researches in South Africa*, Livingstone's book, is published.

ENDNOTES

ARABIA: a largely desert peninsula in southwestern Asia, located between the Persian Gulf and the Red Sea

BIG-GAME: of large wild animals that are often hunted for sport or meat

COLONIES: countries or lands ruled by another country that is usually far away

FIRST OPIUM WAR: the first of two trading wars, it was fought from 1839 to 1842 between Britain and China over Chinese attempts to end the trade of the addictive drug opium within its borders

MALARIA: a disease resulting in fever and chills that is carried by parasites in mosquitoes and transferred to people through mosquito bites

MISSIONARY: a person who travels to another country to spread his or her faith or to do charitable work on behalf of a church

PENTATEUCH: the first five books of the Hebrew Bible; the term comes from the Greek words for five (*penta-*) and book, or implement (*teukhos*)

PLATEAU: an area of high, flat ground

PRINCE HENRY THE NAVIGATOR: a Portuguese prince who sponsored explorations along the western coast of Africa, largely in search of gold and slaves

SEXTANT: an instrument used to determine one's position by measuring the height of the sun or stars above the horizon

TRIBUTE: a gift or payment made in order to guarantee one's safety or protection

TSETSE FLY: a biting fly that feeds on human and animal blood and can transmit a number of diseases, including one known as sleeping sickness

WEST INDIES: a group of islands separating the Atlantic Ocean and Caribbean Sea, located between North and South America

WESTERN: having to do with the western part of the world, particularly Europe and North America

ZANZIBAR: an island in the Indian Ocean off the coast of East Africa that is part of present-day Tanzania

SELECTED BIBLIOGRAPHY

Jeal, Tim. *Livingstone*. New York: G. P. Putnam's Sons, 1973.

Livingstone, David. *Missionary Travels and Researches in South Africa*. London: J. Murray, 1857.

McLynn, Frank. *Hearts of Darkness: The European Exploration of Africa*. New York: Carroll & Graf Publishers, 1993.

Pakenham, Thomas. *The Scramble for Africa: The White Man's Conquest of the Dark Continent from 1876 to 1912*. New York: Random House, 1991.

Reader, John. *Africa: A Biography of the Continent*. New York: Alfred A. Knopf, 1998.

Ross, Andrew. *David Livingstone: Mission and Empire*. New York: Hambledon and London, 2002.

Seaver, George. *David Livingstone: His Life and Letters*. New York: Harper & Brothers, 1957.

Walvin, James. *Atlas of Slavery*. New York: Pearson Longman, 2006.

FOR FURTHER READING

Dugard, Martin. *Into Africa: The Epic Adventures of Stanley & Livingstone*. New York: Doubleday, 2003.

Freedman, Frances. *David Livingstone*. Milwaukee: World Almanac Library, 2002.

Hynson, Colin. *Exploration of Africa*. Mankato, Minn.: NewForest Press, 2011.

Otfinoski, Steven. *David Livingstone: Deep in the Heart of Africa*. New York: Marshall Cavendish Benchmark, 2007.

INDEX

Africa *7, 8, 11, 12, 19, 22, 25, 26, 32*
    animals *12, 25, 26, 32*
    climates *12, 19, 26*
    landscapes *12, 22, 26, 32*
    misconceptions about *11*
    nickname *7*

African Association *12, 14*

the Americas *7, 8, 14*

Angola *25, 41, 44*

Banks, Sir Joseph *12*

Cape Colony (South Africa) *11, 14, 17, 20, 22, 35, 44*

Cape Town *14, 17, 20, 22, 35, 44*

colonies *7, 40*
    see also Angola, Mozambique, Cape Colony

cross-continental expedition *20, 22, 25–26, 27, 29, 32, 33, 35, 40, 41, 44*
    conditions *26, 29*
    dates *22, 25, 29, 32, 35, 44*
    eastward journey *29, 32, 35, 41*
    porters *22, 25, 35, 44*
    preparation for *20, 22, 27*
    supplies *20, 25*
    transportation *25, 32, 35*
    westward journey *25–26, 29, 41*

early explorers in Africa *12, 14, 18*
    Clapperton, Hugh *14*
    Lander, Richard *14*
    Ledyard, John *14*
    Park, Mungo *14*
    Porto, Silva *18*

Egypt *11, 14*

First Opium War *17*

France *8, 14, 40*

Great Britain *7, 8, 14, 17, 20, 23, 29, 35–36, 40, 43, 44*
    and African trading posts *8*
    reception of Livingstone *35–36, 40, 44*
    warships *35, 44*

Kirk, John *39*

Kololo tribe *22, 23, 25, 29, 33, 35, 39, 41, 44*
    King Sekeletu *22, 23, 25, 29, 33, 41*
    Linyanti village *22, 23, 25, 29, 41, 44*
    Pitsane *25, 41*
    Sekwebu *23, 29, 35, 44*

Lake Ngami *18, 44*

Livingstone, Charles *39*

Livingstone, David *7, 9, 13, 14, 17–18, 19, 20, 25–26, 29, 35, 37, 39, 40, 43, 44*
    biographical details *13, 17, 44*
    expedition leader *25–26, 29, 39*
    family *18, 20*
    illnesses *25, 29, 35, 37, 40, 44*
    mission work *17–18*
    promotion of Africa *39, 40*
    writings *9, 19, 26, 37, 39, 44*

Livingstone, Mary Moffat *18, 44*

Lunda tribe *26*
    Chief Shinde *26*

Maclear, Sir Thomas *22, 27*

malaria *12, 25, 29, 33, 35, 39*

mission settlements *14, 17, 22, 25, 32, 39, 40, 44*
    Kuruman *14, 17, 22, 44*

missionaries *7, 13, 14, 17, 18, 28, 36, 39, 44*
    countries represented by *14*
    and London Missionary Society *14, 17, 18, 36, 39*

Moffat, Robert *14, 18*

Mozambique *20, 23, 29, 32, 35, 39, 44*
    Quelimane *23, 35, 44*
    Tete *32*

Murray, Mungo *18, 44*

Nile River *11, 40*
    search for its source *40*

Oswell, William Cotton *18, 44*

Portugal *7, 8, 25, 29, 40*
    and African settlements *7, 25, 29*
    Prince Henry the Navigator *7*

slave trade *8, 11, 20, 26, 40, 43, 44*
    abolishment by Britain *8, 43, 44*
    Livingstone's opposition to *26, 40, 43*

Stanley, Henry Morton *13*

Thornton, Richard *39*

Tswana tribes *17–18, 44*
    Bakhatla people *18, 44*
    Chief Sechele *18*
    Kolobeng village *18*
    Kwena people *18, 44*
    Setswana language *17*

Victoria Falls *29, 32, 44*
    named by Livingstone *29, 44*

Zambezi River *18, 19, 20, 22, 23, 25, 26, 29, 32, 35, 39–40, 41, 44*
    1858 exploration *39–40*
    Kebrabasa Rapids *32, 39, 44*